CRUISING GUIDE
TO INNS AND TAVERNS
NORFOLK BROADS
SIXTH EDITION

by

ROSE LEWIS

British Library Cataloguing in Publication Data
Lewis, Rose

Cruising Guide to Inns and Taverns. Norfolk Broads.
A catalogue record for this book is available from the British Library.

ISBN: 0 9552890 0 9

PUBS WHICH ARE MORE THAN HALF A MILE FROM THE RIVER ARE NOT INCLUDED.

ALL CRUISING TIMES AND DISTANCES ARE APPROXIMATE.

SUMMER TRADING TIMES ARE GENERALLY FROM WHITSUN TO MID SEPTEMBER.

BECAUSE OF THE NEW LAWS REGARDING FACILITIES FOR CHILDREN IT IS BEST TO TELEPHONE AHEAD WHERE THE DESCRIPTION STATES "CHILDREN ARE WELCOME".

FRONT COVER: Approaching Wroxham Bridge
                              from Coltishall
BACK COVER: Map of the Norfolk Broads

Photographs © C W Rose - June 2006

PUBLISHED BY:
Rosec Publications
135 Church Road
Shoeburyness
Essex SS3 9EZ
www.rosec.co.uk

PRINTED IN GREAT BRITAIN BY:
AllStar Services Ltd (Digital Printers)
25 Forward Drive
Christchurch Business Centre
Harrow
HA3 8NT
www.allstar.co.uk
Email: sales@allstar.co.uk

INDEX

IN MEMORY OF MY MOTHER – WITHOUT WHOSE HELP I WOULD NEVER HAVE BEGUN AND OF STEVE - A DEARLY LOVED BROTHER AND BROTHER-IN-LAW WHO PASSED AWAY IN AUGUST 2005.

MY LOVE TO:

CHRIS, MY HUSBAND, FOR BEING MAGNANIMOUS OVER MISSED MEALS, TAKING PHOTOGRAPHS AND DRAWING MAPS WHILST MAKING MOLEHILLS OUT OF ALL MY MOUNTAINS AND MANAGING TO MANOEUVRE AND MOOR WHILST NOT MENTIONING MY NAVIGATIONAL MISHAPS.

IF YOU WISH TO ORDER FUTURE BOOKS, CD-ROMS OR JUST 'AREAS' IN THIS SERIES WE OFFER SECURE ORDERING FACILITIES ON OUR WEB SITE. SAVE MONEY BY ORDERING FROM OUR SITE AT WWW.ROSEC.CO.UK

THE AUTHOR AND PUBLISHERS WELCOME ANY COMMENTS FROM THEIR READERS, GOOD OR BAD. PLEASE SEE THE FRONT PAGE OF THIS BOOK. OUR CUSTOMERS ARE VALUABLE TO US AND WE ARE ALWAYS INTERESTED IN *YOUR* VIEWS.

ROSEC PUBLICATIONS
135 CHURCH ROAD
SHOEBURYNESS
ESSEX SS3 9EZ
www.rosec.co.uk
Email: sales@rosec.co.uk

INTRODUCTION

Unlike the roadways of Britain there are no signposts on the waterways of the Norfolk Broads, one cannot travel after dark and it can take a fair while to "pull up at a pub".

For those who enjoy a decent drink and a good meal in congenial surroundings this river by river guide allows you to see at a glance the choices of venue open to you, the moorings available and the distances and times between your destination, wherever you may find yourself.

After several attempts to navigate our way via various maps and advertisements in an endeavour to discover the welcoming hostelry that must surely be round the next bend in the river, we wrote this Guide - if only to help others "in the same boat".

There are, again, many changes in this Edition. Over the years some of the pubs have closed down or been converted. Where there has been a change of ownership or non-feedback at the time of going to press we have indicated this information on Page 6. Also we have no idea how the new 'no smoking in public places' Bill is going to affect the pubs. Hopefully the new pubs in this book (as well as those that remain) will bring you many happy hours and I can only reiterate what I always say, in my Cruising Guides:

"Have a marvellous holiday and good luck with steering your bedroom to the bar"!

Rose Lewis
June - 2006

PUBS WHO "MISSED THE BOAT"

As it is sometimes difficult to obtain up to date information (either because a pub is changing hands, has closed down or just from sheer lack of interest) between the time of sending our pages to the Printers and a new Edition coming out we have set out below those pubs which are not featured in this edition.

RIVER BURE: Wroxham – The Kings Head Hotel; Horning – Petersfield House Hotel; (sold for housing)
Upton Dyke – The White Horse

RIVER ANT:.. Neatishead – Barton Angler Country Inn; (Private House)   Stalham – Maids Head;
Sutton Staithe– Sutton Staithe Hotel

RIVER THURNE:... Womack Staithe – The Kings Arms

RIVER WAVENEY:... Beccles – The Waveney House Hotel and The Swan House

RIVER YARE:... Buckenham Ferry – Beauchamp Arms; Surlingham – Coldham Hall Tavern

RIVER CHET... Chedgrave – White Horse Inn

We sincerely hope that you are happy with the new pubs that we have introduced into this Edition. Some featured in previous editions some time ago and are now enjoying a face-lift and new Landlords. Some we have left out previously from sheer lack of space – hence the fact that you will find some pubs in this edition sharing a page.

Updates will be available from our website at www.rosec.co.uk. Please feel free to print the update page out. Keep the feedback coming – it has been invaluable to us in the past. Last but not least – we have been tardy in producing this 6th edition but it has not always been easy. Enjoy.

Rosec Publications

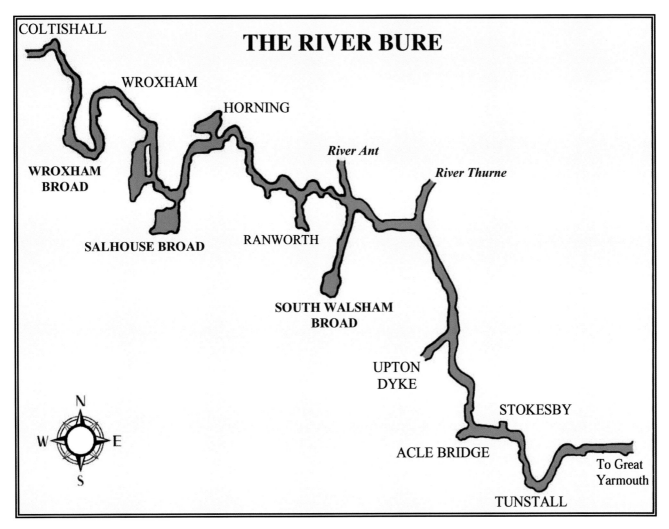

THE RIVER BURE

COLTISHALL
WROXHAM
HORNING
River Ant
River Thurne
WROXHAM BROAD
SALHOUSE BROAD
RANWORTH
SOUTH WALSHAM BROAD
UPTON DYKE
STOKESBY
ACLE BRIDGE
To Great Yarmouth
TUNSTALL

N
W E
S

THE RIVER BURE - DISTANCES AND TIMINGS

COLTISHALL TO GREAT YARMOUTH

COLTISHALL TO WROXHAM = 4 MILES - 45 MINUTES
WROXHAM TO HORNING = 5 MILES - 1 HOUR
HORNING TO RANWORTH = 3 MILES - 30 MINUTES
RANWORTH TO THURNE MOUTH = 3 MILES - 30 MINUTES
(ANT MOUTH TO THURNE MOUTH = 2 MILES - 20 MINUTES)
THURNE MOUTH TO UPTON DYKE = 3 MILES - 30 MINUTES
UPTON DYKE TO ACLE BRIDGE = 1 MILE -20 MINUTES
ACLE BRIDGE TO STOKESBY = 2 MILES - 20 MINUTES
STOKESBY TO TUNSTALL = 2 MILES - 20 MINUTES
TUNSTALL TO GREAT YARMOUTH = 7 MILES -1 1/2 HOURS

GREAT YARMOUTH TO COLTISHALL

GREAT YARMOUTH TO TUNSTALL = 7 MILES - 1 1/2 HOURS
TUNSTALL TO STOKESBY = 2 MILES - 20 MINUTES
STOKESBY TO ACLE BRIDGE = 2 MILES - 20 MINUTES
ACLE BRIDGE TO UPTON DYKE = 1 MILE - 20 MINUTES
UPTON DYKE TO THURNE MOUTH = 3 MILES - 30 MINUTES
(THURNE MOUTH TO ANT MOUTH = 2 MILES - 20 MINUTES)
THURNE MOUTH TO RANWORTH = 3 MILES - 30 MINUTES
RANWORTH TO HORNING = 3 MILES - 30 MINUTES
HORNING TO WROXHAM = 5 MILES - 1 HOUR
WROXHAM TO COLTISHALL = 4 MILES - 45 MINUTES

THE RIVER BURE

COLTISHALL IS THE HEAD OF NAVIGATION ON THIS RIVER WHICH RUNS FOR OVER 30 MILES DOWN TO GREAT YARMOUTH. ONE OF THE PRETTIEST STRETCHES ON THE BROADS IS FROM COLTISHALL TO WROXHAM. GOOD FOOD AT THE "KINGS HEAD."

WROXHAM BRIDGE (BUILT IN 1614) MUST ONLY BE NAVIGATED AT LOW TIDES. (HEIGHT 7'3" AT HIGH WATER). WROXHAM IS ONE OF THE BEST PLACES TO SHOP AND FROM HERE YOU CAN VISIT WROXHAM BARNS OR TAKE A 9 MILE TRIP ON THE BURE VALLEY RAILWAY TO AYLSHAM.

BEFORE REACHING HORNING YOU PASS WROXHAM BROAD, HOVETON GREAT BROAD NATURE TRAIL, SALHOUSE BROAD AND SALHOUSE VILLAGE WHERE THERE IS AN EQUESTRIAN CENTRE. HORNING STRETCHES FOR QUITE A WAY AND YOU MAY SEE THE "SOUTHERN COMFORT" PADDLE STEAMER PLYING BACK AND FORTH BETWEEN HERE AND RANWORTH DYKE ALMOST OPPOSITE THE ANT MOUTH. THE ENTRANCE TO RANWORTH LIES THROUGH MALTHOUSE BROAD.

THE DISTANCE BETWEEN THE ANT MOUTH AND THE THURNE MOUTH IS TWO MILES. TWO MILES FURTHER ON IS THE ENTRANCE TO UPTON DYKE ON YOUR RIGHT – THE "WHITE HORSE" PUB IS A TEN MINUTE WALK UP THROUGH THE VILLAGE. ACLE BRIDGE COMES NEXT AND THEN STOKESBY WITH ITS CANDLEMAKING AND MODEL CENTRE.

ON NOW TO TUNSTALL WHICH IS THE LAST PLACE TO MOOR BEFORE THE STRETCH TO GREAT YARMOUTH (MOORINGS PICTURED ABOVE) WHERE NUMEROUS ATTRACTIONS MAY KEEP YOU ENTERTAINED FOR A WHILE. HORSE DRAWN CARRIAGES, TREASURE WORLD, CRAZY GOLF, THE HOUSE OF WAX, REGENT BOWL (TEN PIN BOWLING), WELLINGTON AND BRITANNIA PIERS, MARINA LEISURE CENTRE, PLEASURE BEACH FAIRGROUND, RIPLEY'S ODDITORIUM, THE SEA LIFE CENTRE, BUTTERFLY FARM AND MERRIVALE MODEL VILLAGE ARE ALL NEARBY. THERE ARE ALSO MANY EXCELLENT PUBS AND RESTAURANTS (TRY "THE ALBATROSS" (01493 858030) AND THE "SAVOY"(ENGLISH, GREEK & CONTINENTAL CUISINE – 01493 332727) BOTH IN REGENT ROAD.

COLTISHALL

THE KINGS HEAD
TEL: (01603) 737426

4 MILES TO WROXHAM - 45 MINUTES

MOORINGS: These are plentiful and side on. There is no charge for the first 24 hours and you will find the Kings Head tucked just behind the Rising Sun, on your left as you approach the main road.

SUMMER:	11 to 3 and 6 to 11
WINTER:	11 to 3 and 6 to 11
SUNDAY:	All day

BEERS: Adnams, Woodfordes and Courage, Draught Guinness and Draught Extra Cold Guinness.

LAGERS: Kronenberg, Carlsberg, Fosters, 1664

SPECIALITIES: Herring Roes. Cromer Crab. Calves Liver and Crispy Bacon. Cutlet of 'Old Spot' Pork. Vegetarian Meals. Breakfast served from 07.30 to 09.30.

SUNDAY LUNCH: £6.95 per head

BAR MEALS: Noon to 2 and 7 to 9.30

DINING FACILITIES: Seating for 60. Times as above. Typical cost of three course meal for two with wine: £50.

CARDS: All main cards accepted.

A 17th century beamed interior with Broadland antique and fishing themes running throughout the pub. Log fires are lit when it's cool. A tropical fish aquarium adds a nice touch

The no smoking Restaurant which overlooks the seating provided outside and the river beyond has been totally refurbished and extended. A very extensive menu makes this a popular place to eat, especially at weekends, so it is best to call ahead.

Sorry, no dogs allowed. Good facilities for the disabled. Ensuite bedrooms available.

COLTISHALL

THE NEW RISING SUN   TEL: (01603) 737440

4 MILES TO WROXHAM - 45 MINUTES

MOORINGS: Approximately 35 side on. There is no fee for the first 24 hours and the pub is 50 to 500 yards away.

SUMMER:	All day
WINTER:	All day
SUNDAY:	All day

BEERS:	Straw Dog, IPA, Wherry, Guinness, John Smiths, Deuchars IPA and Guests.
LAGERS:	Fosters, Stella and 1664

SPECIALITIES: Monkfish. Squid. Beef Wellington. Steaks. Beefburgers. Vegetarian and Childrens' Menu. OAP specials.

SUNDAY LUNCH: Carvery - £6.95

BAR MEALS: Noon to 9 (Summer) and Noon to 2 and 6 to 9 (Winter).

DINING FACILITIES: Seating for 60. Meal times as above. Typical cost of three course meal for two with wine: £25.

CARDS: All main cards accepted, plus Cashback.

Situated on an old public staithe once used by traditional Norfolk Wherries this is a well known hostelry - originally a grain store and maltings.

Renamed and smartened up the pub still retains it's character. A rambling interior, with interesting photographs of the old days in the two bars. Music is supplied and pool is available. Sorry, no dogs.

An extremely large patio lies adjacent to a play area. Children are also welcome in the restaurant which overlooks the river and is a no-smoking area. Occasional jazz nights during the summer months. Excellent facilities for the disabled.

COLTISHALL

THE RED LION   TEL: (01603) 737402

4 MILES TO WROXHAM - 45 MINUTES

MOORINGS: These are plentiful and side on. There is no charge for the first 24 hours. Turn left at the top of the staithe, walk past the small parade of shops in the village and you will find the pub 400 yards up the road almost opposite the church. Torches required at night.

SUMMER:	11 to 3 and 5 to 11. All day Saturday.
WINTER:	11 to 3 and 5 to 11
SUNDAY:	All day
BEERS:	Tetleys, Boddingtons, Spitfire, Adnams, Guinness and Couteshall Weaselpis
LAGERS:	Carlsberg and Stella Artois
SPECIALITIES:	BBQ Ribs. Omelettes. Chilli Con Carne. Steak and Ale Pie. Cromer Crab. Pizzas. Childrens' Menu. Specials Board.
SUNDAY LUNCH:	Roasts - £6.95.
BAR MEALS:	5 to 9.30 p.m.

DINING FACILITIES: Seating for 60. Food available from 5 to 9.30 p.m. Typical cost of three course meal for two with wine: £25.

CARDS: All main cards, plus Cashback.

A quaint split level pub which was originally three Alms Houses and a very small beer house dating back to the 14th Century.

Families are sure of good food and a warm welcome. Please note that the restaurant is non-smoking. Dogs are allowed, in the 'small' bar. Good facilites for the disabled.

In the two oak beamed bars, the real ales available will lure the traditional beer drinkers even if they failed to take note of one of the beers mentioned above which is brewed exclusively for the Red Lion!

HORNING

THE SWAN HOTEL   TEL: (01692) 630316

5 MILES FROM WROXHAM - 1 HOUR
3 MILES TO RANWORTH - 30 MINUTES

MOORINGS: Approximately 10 side on. There is no charge and the hotel is across the lawns.

SUMMER:	All day
WINTER:	All day
SUNDAY:	Noon to 10.30

BEERS: John Smiths, Greene King IPA, Guinness and Guest Ales

LAGERS: Stella, Carlsberg and Carling Extra Cold

SPECIALITIES: Cottage Pie. Mixed Grill. Rump and Sirloin Steaks. Vegetarian and Childrens' Menu. One course meal £4.99. 2 - £6.49 and a three course meal for £7.99.

SUNDAY LUNCH: Roasts - £7.50

BAR MEALS: 11.30 to 10. Noon to 10 on Sundays.

DINING FACILITIES: Seating for 44. Times as above Typical cost of three course meal for two with wine: £25.

CARDS: All main cards accepted.

Long and rambling this hotel was built in 1897. Generous seating is provided in the gardens which front onto the river. Catch the 'Southern Comfort' Paddle Steamer from outside the hotel.

Settle yourself anywhere for a meal. An off-set dining area is offered which is a no-smoking area. Pool is provided and there is a 'games' area. Dogs are allowed in the gardens. Family entertainment is regularly organised. Very good facilities for the disabled. Excellent 'specials' blackboard.

En Suite rooms are available for bed and breakfast. Please telephone ahead for details.

HORNING

THE NEW INN   TEL: (01692) 631223

4 1/2 MILES FROM WROXHAM - 1 HOUR
3 MILES TO RANWORTH - 45 MINUTES

MOORINGS: Mooring for about 12 boats – stern on. Distance to the pub is 25 yards.

SUMMER:	10.30 a.m. to 11 p.m.
WINTER:	10.30 a.m. to 11 p.m.
SUNDAY:	11 a.m. to 10.30 p.m.

BEERS:	John Smiths, Nelsons Revenge, Adnams, Green King IPA, Dark Mild and Guinness
LAGERS:	Fosters, Stella and 1664.

SPECIALITIES: Fresh Cromer Crab. Steak and Ale Pie. Steak and Stilton Pie. Minted Lamb. Beef Lasagne. Vegetarian and Childrens' Menu. Liqueur Coffees and Speciality Ices. Breakfast between 8 and 10 a.m.

SUNDAY LUNCH: £7.25

BAR MEALS: Noon to 3. Not evenings.

DINING FACILITIES: Seating for 30. Noon to 8 p.m.. Typical cost of a two course meal for two with wine: £30

CARDS: All main cards accepted.

The oldest pub in Horning and privately owned for four years, this establishment has recently been extensively renovated and now has a large, extremely attractive, riverside garden, where a play area for children and. pool tables are available.

The New Inn is famous for the antiquities and memorabilia inside the two bars and has been featured on TV and BBC holiday programmes.

Smoking and non-smoking areas throughout. Limited facilities for the disabled. Sorry – no dogs except guide dogs allowed inside. Call ahead to reserve a mooring in busy times.

HORNING

THE FERRY INN   TEL: (01692) 630259

5 ½ MILES FROM WROXHAM - 1 HOUR
2 ½ MILES TO RANWORTH - 30 MINUTES

MOORINGS: There are a number of moorings all around Horning proper but outside the pub there is room for about 20 side on. A charge of £5 after 5 p.m. is levied on the pub side but moor on the other side and you can be rowed over.

SUMMER:	All day
WINTER:	All day
SUNDAY:	All day
BEERS:	John Smiths , Theakstons Mild, Woodfordes Wherry, IPA and Guinness plus two Guest Beers.
LAGERS:	Fosters, Stella, Carling and 1664.
SPECIALITIES:	Duck with Rustic Orange Sauce. Smoky Haddock. Bubble and Squeak. Fish Pies. Minted Lamb. Cod and Prawn Mornay. Beef and Ale Pie. Vegetarian and Childrens' Menu.
SUNDAY LUNCH:	Roasts- £6.95
BAR MEALS:	11 a.m. to 9 p.m.

DINING FACILITIES: Seating for 100. Times as above. Average cost of two course meal for two with wine: £30.

CARDS: All major cards and ATM.

RANWORTH

MALTSTERS   TEL: (01603) 270241

3 MILES FROM HORNING - 30 MINUTES
1 MILE TO ANT MOUTH - 20 MINUTES
3 MILES TO THURNE MOUTH - 30 MINUTES
6 MILES TO ACLE BRIDGE– 1 HOUR

MOORINGS: Approximtely 20, stern on. There is no charge for the first 24 hours and the distance to the pub is 100 to 200 yards. A busy spot so moor early to avoid the rush.

SUMMER:	All day
WINTER:	All day
SUNDAY:	All day
BEERS:	Theakstons Mild, John Smiths, Guinness, Woodfordes Wherry and IPA.
LAGERS:	Carling and Stella.
SPECIALITIES:	Lasagne. Beef 'n Ale Pie. Mushrooms and Rarebit. Fishcakes. Curries. Pasta. Vegetarian and Childrens' Menu.
SUNDAY LUNCH:	Main Menu available.
BAR MEALS:	Noon to 9 – Monday to Saturday Noon to 8.30 on Sundays

DINING FACILITIES: Seating for 40. Times as above. Typical cost of two course meal for two with wine: £25.

CARDS: All main cards plus ATM.

ACLE BRIDGE

THE BRIDGE   TEL: (01493) 750288

**6 MILES FROM RANWORTH – 1 HOUR
2 MILES TO STOKESBY - 20 MINUTES**

MOORINGS: Numerous on both sides of the river. There is a charge of £4 for overnight moorings from 6 p.m. onwards. Distance to pub is 75 to 200 yards. Torches useful at night.

SUMMER:	11.30 to 11
WINTER:	11.30 to 3 and 6 to 11
SUNDAY:	Noon to 11

BEERS:	Adnams, Guinness, Green King IPA, John Smiths and Woodfordes Wherry.
LAGERS:	Fosters, Kronenberg, Stella and Carling

SPECIALITIES: Cottage Pie. Lamb Stew and dumplings. Moussaka. Apple Crumble. Baguettes. Vegetarian and Childrens' Menu.

SUNDAY LUNCH: Carvery Roasts - £6.95

BAR MEALS: During opening hours .

DINING FACILITIES: Seating for 100 anywhere in pub and in non-smoking Dining Area. Times as above. Typical cost of two course meal for two with wine: £25.

CARDS: All main cards welcome, except Amex.

STOKESBY

THE FERRY INN   TEL: (01493) 751096

**2 MILES FROM ACLE BRIDGE – 20 MINUTES
2 MILES TO TUNSTALL – 20 MINUTES**

MOORINGS: Outside the pub there is room for 10 or so boats and mooring is free. A £5 fee for 24 hours is collected further downstream. Distance to the pub is 50 to 200 yards. Keep and eye on the rise and fall of the river.

SUMMER:	All day
WINTER:	All day
SUNDAY:	All day

BEERS:	Adnams, Guinness and Guest Ales.
LAGERS:	Carlsberg and Bitburger.

SPECIALITIES: All day breakfast. Braised lamb shank. Home made cheesecakes..Childrens' and Vegetarian Menu.

SUNDAY LUNCH: Roasts - £5.99.

BAR MEALS: 11.30 to 2.30 and 6 to 9 Mon-Saturday Noon to 3 and 6 to 9 on Sunday.

DINING FACILITIES: Seating anywhere. Times as above. Average cost of two course meal for two with wine: £25.

CARDS: Main cards accepted.

TUNSTALL

THE PONTIAC ROAD HOUSE TEL: (01493) 750263

2 MILES FROM STOKESBY FERRY – 20 MINUTES
7 MILES TO GREAT YARMOUTH – 1 ½ HOURS

MOORINGS: Plentiful and just outside the pub which is on your right as you go downstream to Great Yarmouth. There is no charge. Torches useful at night Previously known as the 'Stracey Arms', then 'The Feathers', then the 'Pink Cadillac'. Possibility of change of ownership in 2007.

SUMMER:	All day
WINTER:	All day
SUNDAY:	All day
BEERS:	John Smiths and Guinness plus Guest Ales
LAGERS:	Stella Artois, Fosters and 1664.

SPECIALITIES: Breakfast (9.30 to 11.30). Tiger Prawns. Surf and Turf. Beef Ribs. Battered Cod. Mushroom Stroganoff. Chargrilled Steaks and Chicken. Texan Sizzlers.

SUNDAY LUNCH: Roasts - £7.95 - £4.95 for children.

BAR MEALS: Noon to 9

DINING FACILITIES: 70 in the non-smoking restaurant. Times as above. Average cost of three course meal for two with wine: £35.

CARDS: Main cards accepted.

Totally renovated to a very high standard with excellent facilities for the disabled and extremely pleasant gardens and a large Patio area where BBQs are held in the summer months. Pool table. Children welcome. TV.

The 'spinning' Statue of Liberty may surprise you as will the 1947 Pontiac Silver Streak which George Michael commissioned to be totally covered in segments of mirror. Framed 45s with photos of the Artists for sale.

Friday night 'Acts' and 'Legends'. Win the T Shirt – see if you can accept the 'Road House Steak Challenge'!

GREAT YARMOUTH

THE WHITE SWAN   TEL: (01493) 842027

7 MILES FROM TUNSTALL – 1 ½ HOURS
4 MILES TO BREYDON WATER'S END – 30 MINUTES

MOORINGS: Moorings at the Yacht Station are free for the first hour, £5 for 12 hours and £10 for 24 hours. All side on and the Harbour Master keeps an eye on your rope security with regard to the rise and fall of the river here.

SUMMER:	All day
WINTER:	All day
SUNDAY:	All day

BEERS: John Smiths Smooth and Cask, Spitfire, Courage Dark Mild and Guinness
LAGERS: Carlsberg, 1664, Stella and Fosters.

SPECIALITIES: Mixed Grill. Griddled Gammon and Steaks. Home made Chilli, Steak 'n Ale Pie. Cottage Pie. Lasagne. Childrens' Menu. Mon-Sat - Specials plus free pint!

SUNDAY LUNCH: Roasts - £5.95 – two courses.

BAR MEALS: 11.30 to 2.30 and 5 to 8.30-ish.

DINING FACILITIES: Seating for 40. Average cost of two course meal for two with wine: £25.

CARDS: All main cards accepted. Minimum spend £5.

Completely refurbished a few years ago this pub now offers two large bars. It's a pub for families with outside seating, pool, 'games' machines and a jukebox.

Dogs are allowed in the public bar. Quizzes on Sunday nights during summer months.

The building is over 400 years old and in the 18th century it saw a bizarre turn of events when a high masted ship sank by the bridge and the drowned bodies were laid out there to be counted. Not surprisingly there are various tales of hauntings to this day. Ask the Staff about the 'trapdoor'.

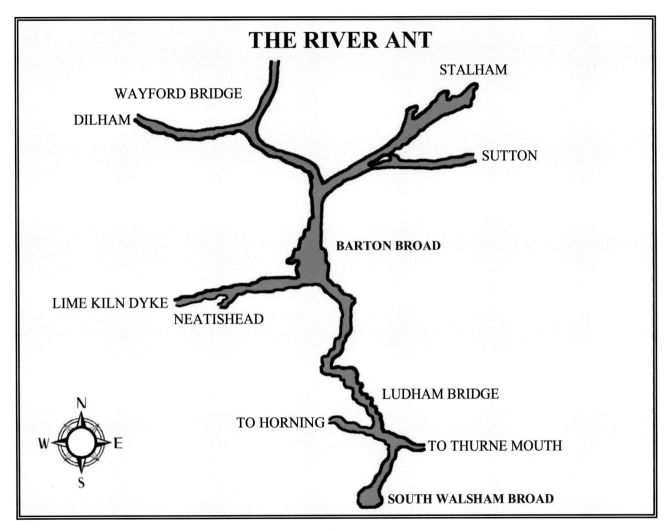

THE RIVER ANT

STALHAM

WAYFORD BRIDGE

DILHAM

SUTTON

BARTON BROAD

LIME KILN DYKE

NEATISHEAD

LUDHAM BRIDGE

TO HORNING

N
W E
S

TO THURNE MOUTH

SOUTH WALSHAM BROAD

THE RIVER ANT - DISTANCES AND TIMINGS

MOUTH OF THE ANT TO NEATISHEAD, WAYFORD BRIDGE, DILHAM, SUTTON STAITHE AND STALHAM

MOUTH OF ANT TO LUDHAM BRIDGE = 1 MILE - 20 MINUTES
LUDHAM BRIDGE TO NEATISHEAD = 5 MILES - 1 HOUR
NEATISHEAD TO STALHAM OR SUTTON STAITHE = 3 MILES - 45 MINUTES
NEATISHEAD TO WAYFORD BRIDGE = 3 MILES - 45 MINUTES
WAYFORD BRIDGE TO STALHAM OR SUTTON STAITHE = 3 MILES - 45 MINUTES
WAYFORD BRIDGE TO DILHAM = 1 MILE - 20 MINUTES

DILHAM, WAYFORD BRIDGE, STALHAM, SUTTON STAITHE AND NEATISHEAD TO MOUTH OF THE ANT

DILHAM TO WAYFORD BRIDGE = 1 MILE - 20 MINUTES
WAYFORD BRIDGE TO NEATISHEAD = 3 MILES - 45 MINUTES
STALHAM OR SUTTON STAITHE TO WAYFORD BRIDGE = 3 MILES - 45 MINUTES
STALHAM OR SUTTON STAITHE TO NEATISHEAD = 3 MILES - 45 MINUTES
NEATISHEAD TO LUDHAM BRIDGE = 5 MILES - 1 HOUR
LUDHAM BRIDGE TO MOUTH OF ANT = 1 MILE - 20 MINUTES

RIVER ANT

AN EXTREMELY POPULAR RIVER DURING THE FISHING SEASON. THE MOUTH OF THE RIVER ANT LIES BETWEEN, AND ON THE OPPOSITE SIDE TO, RANWORTH BROAD AND SOUTH WALSHAM BROAD ON THE BURE. AT LUDHAM BRIDGE YOU WILL FIND GOOD MOORINGS TO YOUR RIGHT AND LEFT, AND LUDHAM BRIDGE SERVICES, ON THE RIGHT BANK, IS A GOOD PLACE FOR VICTUALS.

CRUISING UPSTREAM YOU WILL PASS HOW HILL NATURE RESERVE ON YOUR RIGHT. HERE YOU WILL FIND TOAD HOLE COTTAGE WHERE YOU CAN BUY TICKETS FOR THE "ELECTRIC EEL", A NOISELESS BOAT FROM WHICH YOU CAN SEE THE NUMEROUS WILDLIFE ON THE WATER TRAIL.

CROSSING BARTON BROAD, AS YOU GO UPSTREAM, KEEP ALL RED STAKES TO YOUR LEFT, AND TO YOUR RIGHT WHEN RETURNING. YOU CAN PASS EITHER SIDE OF PLEASURE HILL ISLAND WHICH IS SOON TO BE ENTIRELY REBUILT AS A LANDMARK. TO CRUISE TO NEATISHEAD KEEP TO THE LEFT AS YOU ENTER THE BROAD AND TAKE THE FIRST MAIN LEFT FORK. TO VISIT BARTON TURF GO ACROSS THE BROAD AND TAKE THE LEFT FORK WHERE INDICATED. TO GO TO WAYFORD BRIDGE (HEIGHT AT HIGH WATER 7') AND DILHAM, KEEP TO THE LEFT FORK. FOR STALHAM OR SUTTON BEAR RIGHT WHERE INDICATED FURTHER UPSTREAM BEARING LEFT FOR STALHAM, RIGHT FOR SUTTON.

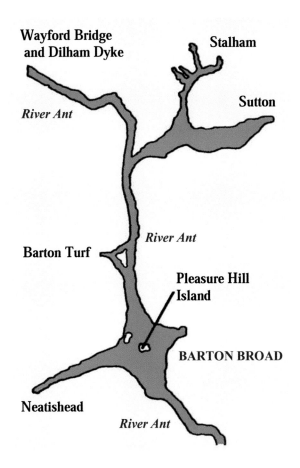

LUDHAM BRIDGE

DOG INN TEL: (01692) 630321

1 MILE FROM ANT MOUTH – 20 MINUTES
4 ½ MILES TO NEATISHEAD – 1 HOUR

MOORINGS: Although you cannot see the pub from the river it is only ¼ mile walk from the Bridge – past the tea shop. No charge for the numerous side on moorings on both banks.

SUMMER:	Noon to 11
WINTER:	Noon to 11
SUNDAY:	Noon to 10.30

BEERS: John Smiths and constantly changing range of local Real Ales. Grapefruit Ale in Summer is very popular.

LAGERS: Fosters and Kronenbourg.

SPECIALITIES: Roast Partridge. Lemon Sole. Cromer Crab. The local Butcher's Sausages are a great favourite.

SUNDAY LUNCH: Roasts - £6.95

BAR MEALS: Noon to 2 and 6 to 9

DINING FACILITIES: Dining Room. Times as above. Typical cost of two course meal for two with wine: £20.

CARDS: All main cards accepted.

A change of ownership in 2004. Good service here in lively and cheerful surroundings with pleasant background music. A dart board and pool table are available in the childrens room

Open fires in Winter and large gardens to the front with generous seating. Good facilities for the disabled. Dogs allowed if kept on leads

Smoking is not permitted in the Dining Room but plenty of garden seating as above.

From here the remains of St. Benet's Abbey and How Hill Nature Reserve can be reached by road and footpath.

NEATISHEAD

THE WHITE HORSE TEL: (01692) 630828

5 MILES FROM LUDHAM BRIDGE - 1 HOUR
3 MILES TO STALHAM OR SUTTON STAITHE - 45 MINUTES
3 MILES TO WAYFORD BRIDGE - 45 MINUTES

MOORINGS: Several, side on, in Lime Kiln Dyke. These are free for 24 hours and are 300 yards from the pub. You can also moor at Gay's Staithe and walk the ½ mile to the pub. Torches required at night.

SUMMER:	All day
WINTER:	All day
SUNDAY:	Noon to 11

BEERS:	Greene King, IPA, Tetleys, Guinness, Adnams and Broadside
LAGERS:	Stella, Carlsberg and Fosters.
SPECIALITIES:	Dover Sole. Pan Fried Mushrooms. 10 oz Filet Steak. Mixed Grill. OAPs' Set Menu Childrens' Menu.
SUNDAY LUNCH:	Roasts - £5.95
BAR MEALS:	12 to 2.30 and 6 to 9

DINING FACILITIES: Seating in any of the 3 bars (one of which is non-smoking) and sheltered terrace. Times as above. Typical cost of two course meal for two with wine: £25.

This 500 year old hostelry is now under new management..Much of the pub has been left in it's original state, with bare floors and small bars – a refreshing change in this era of plastic and chrome. Smoking and non-smoking areas throughout.

Darts, cribbage, pool, table football and a warm welcome. Live music during regattas and holiday weekends. Children welcome in the lounge bar and restaurant. Limited facilities for the disabled. Dogs allowed in the terrace area. Take time to read the little bronze plaques everywhere.

Lime Kiln Dyke is an attractive wooded area with a turning basin at its apex.

WAYFORD BRIDGE

WAYFORD BRIDGE HOTEL TEL: (01692) 582414

3 MILES FROM NEATISHEAD - 45 MINUTES
3 MILES TO STALHAM OR SUTTON STAITHE - 45 MINUTES
1 MILE TO DILHAM - 20 MINUTES

MOORINGS: Numerous on both banks either side of the bridge. A nominal fee is payable after 5.30 if staying overnight on the West bank. Distance to the pub is 50 to 300 yards. Torches useful at night.

SUMMER:	11 to 2.30 and 5.30 to 11
WINTER:	11 to 2.30 and 5.30 to 11
SUNDAY:	12 to 2 and 6 to 11.

BEERS:	Worthington, Adnams, M&B Mild Caffreys, Guinness & Guests
LAGERS:	Stella, Carling and Grolsch

SPECIALITIES: Fresh Fish and Charcoal Grilled Specials. Tagliatelli Carbonara. Childrens' and Vegetarian Menus. Specials Menu.

SUNDAY LUNCH: Roasts - £6.95

BAR MEALS: Noon to 2 and 6 to 9

DINING FACILITIES: Seating for over 100. Times as above. Typical cost of three course meal for two with wine: £30.

CARDS: All main cards accepted.

Once known as the Woodfarm Inn this has been taken turned into a lovely hotel. There are 12, very large, en-suite rooms with those on the ground floor suitable for people with mobility problems. Children and dogs welcome.

The tiled, circular bar with it's plush seating and mellow cream walls boasts oak beams, farming implements and copper canopies over the fireplaces..

Two non-smoking restaurants (Bistro and A La Carte) command excellent views of the river. Good for fishing all round this area..

DILHAM DYKE

THE CROSS KEYS TEL: (01692) 536398

1 MILE FROM WAYFORD BRIDGE- 20 MINUTES

MOORINGS: There are 4 to 5 side on and there is no fee. Make your way up the grass embankment and turn left at the Bridge. The pub is a five minute walk away.

SUMMER:	11.30 to 3 and 6 to 11
WINTER:	Noon to 2.30 and 7 to 11
SUNDAY:	Noon to 4 and 6 to 10.30

Times may change so please telephone ahead

BEERS: Adnams Bitter and Broadside. Greene King, John Smiths and Guinness

LAGERS: Stella Artois and Carlsberg

SPECIALITIES: Garlic Tiger Prawns. Chicken Leek and Stilton Pie. Tagliatelli. Chilli Con Carne. Brie Rosti. Omelettes. 'Specials'.

SUNDAY LUNCH: Traditional Roasts. £5.50.

BAR MEALS: Noon to 2 and 7 to 9

DINING FACILITIES: Seating for 30. Times as above. Typical cost of two course meal for two with wine: £20.

CARDS: Cheque with bankers cards.

One of the more delightful village inns with one bar overlooking the bowling green. Pleasant hospitality and a convivial atmosphere make this an agreeable stopover for the traveller who seeks that away from it all mood, without mooring in the middle of a Broad.

Pool and darts are provided in the saloon bar. Children alllowed in the garden. Dogs on leads, please. Log burning stove. TV in the public bar.

An extremely attractive 3 mph stretch of river leads to the end of navigation on the River Ant. Please take care in your approach along this stretch to avoid wash against the riverside gardens of private houses. Watch for Kingfishers!

STALHAM

THE GREBE　　TEL: (01692) 580376

3 MILES FROM NEATISHEAD - 45 MINUTES
3 MILES TO WAYFORD BRIDGE - 45 MINUTES

MOORINGS: Numerous free areas in and around the various boatyards and Stalham Dyke. The pub is the middle one you will come to, on your right, in the High Street which is a five minute stroll away.

SUMMER:	All day
WINTER:	11 to 3 and 7 to 11 (All day Saturday)
SUNDAY:	Noon to 11

BEERS:	John Smiths Smooth, Greene King and Caffreys
LAGERS:	Stella, Fosters and Carling.

There is no food available in the Grebe but since the pub has not been in the book since the 3rd edition it was felt that it deserved a mention.

*A family **pub** which offers a beer garden, pool table and live entertainment at weekends. Also SKY is available here. Dogs allowed. Limited facilities for the disabled.*

The Grebe is fondly remembered by Bob Fisher of Yachts and Yachting fame.

STALHAM

THE KINGFISHER HOTEL　　TEL: (01692) 581974

3 MILES FROM NEATISHEAD - 45 MINUTES
3 MILES TO WAYFORD BRIDGE - 45 MINUTES

MOORINGS: Numerous free areas in and around the various boatyards and Stalham Dyke. The pub is at the top of the High Street - approximately 1/4 mile from the moorings.

SUMMER:	11 to 2.30 and 6 to 11
WINTER:	11 to 2.30 and 6 to 11
SUNDAY:	12 to 2.30 and 7 to 10.30

BEERS:	M&B Mild, Greene King, Worthington, Guinness and Caffreys
LAGERS:	Grolsch and Carling Black Label
SPECIALITIES:	Mussels. Braised Beef Casserole. Panfried Boneless Loin of Pork in Mushroom and Stilton Sauce. Skate. Vegetarian and Childrens' Menus.
SUNDAY LUNCH:	Roasts - £4.95
BAR MEALS:	Noon to 2 and 7 to 9

DINING FACILITIES: Seating for 40. Noon to 2 and 7 to 9. Typical cost of three course meal for two with wine: £35.

CARDS: All major cards accepted.

STALHAM

THE SWAN   TEL: (01692) 582829

3 MILES FROM NEATISHEAD - 45 MINUTES
3 MILES TO WAYFORD BRIDGE - 45 MINUTES

MOORINGS: Numerous free areas in and around the various boatyards and Stalham Dyke. The pub is on your left just before The Grebe.

SUMMER:	All day
WINTER:	All day
SUNDAY:	Noon to 11

BEERS: Adnams Ales, John Smiths Bitter, Murphys and Guinness.

LAGERS: Stella, Carlsberg and Carling Extra Cold.

SPECIALITIES: Toasted Sandwiches and Hot Baguettes. Burgers and Omelettes. Huge, 'all day' Breakfast for £5.95. Scampi, Cod and Plaice. Lasagne and Chilli Con Carne. Daily Specials.

SUNDAY LUNCH: Roasts - £4.95.

BAR MEALS: 11 to 9 (Noon to 9 on Sundays)

DINING FACILITIES: Seating for 20 and anywhere in pub. Times as for bar meals. Average cost for two for a main meal with wine: £20

CARDS: All main cards accepted.

A sociable and welcoming pub where the lounge bar is wood panelled and has warm red furnishings, soft lighting and background music.

The public bar offers a pool table whilst the oak panelled lounge bar has comfortable seating. The small, non-smoking dining room has an inglenook fireplace Good access for wheelchairs to all areas.

Dogs allowed except in the restaurant. Children under 16 are allowed in the lounge area and restaurant only. Weekend entertainment and Sky.

THE RIVER THURNE - DISTANCES AND TIMINGS

MOUTH OF THE THURNE TO HICKLING, HORSEY AND WEST SOMERTON

MOUTH OF THE THURNE TO THURNE = 1/2 MILE - 15 MINUTES
THURNE TO WOMACK STAITHE = 2 MILES - 20 MINUTES
WOMACK STAITHE TO POTTER HEIGHAM = 2 MILES - 20 MINUTES
POTTER HEIGHAM TO HICKLING BROAD = 4 1/2 MILES - 1 HOUR
POTTER HEIGHAM TO WEST SOMERTON = 4 1/2 MILES - 1 HOUR
POTTER HEIGHAM TO HORSEY MERE = 4 MILES - 1 HOUR

HICKLING, HORSEY AND WEST SOMERTON TO MOUTH OF THE THURNE

HORSEY MERE TO POTTER HEIGHAM = 4 MILES - 1 HOUR
WEST SOMERTON TO POTTER HEIGHAM = 4 1/2 MILES - 1 HOUR
HICKLING BROAD TO POTTER HEIGHAM = 4 1/2 MILES - 1 HOUR
POTTER HEIGHAM TO WOMACK STAITHE = 2 MILES - 20 MINUTES
WOMACK STAITHE TO THURNE = 2 MILES - 20 MINUTES
THURNE TO MOUTH OF THE THURNE = 1/2 MILE - 15 MINUTES

THE RIVER THURNE

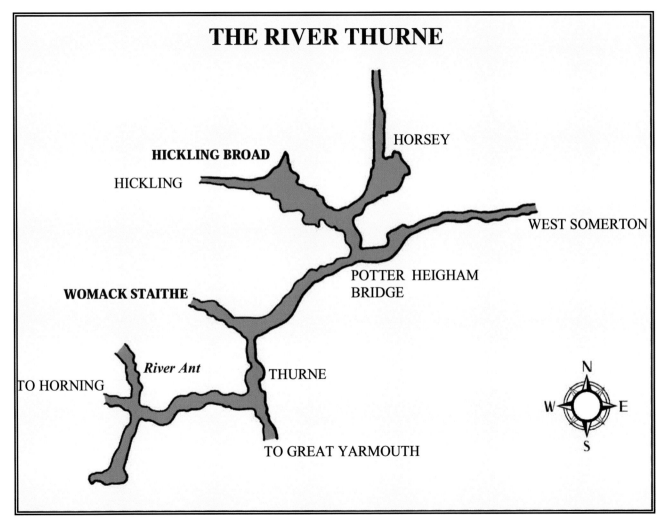

THE RIVER THURNE

JUST PAST THE MOUTH OF THE THURNE IS ST. BENET'S LEVEL WINDPUMP ON YOUR LEFT AND THURNE DYKE WINDPUMP ON YOUR RIGHT, WHICH IS OPEN DURING DAYLIGHT HOURS IN THE SUMMER.

IF YOU VISIT WOMACK STAITHE (WALK FROM MOORINGS TO LUDHAM) YOU'LL SEE THE NORFOLK WHERRY TRUST. ON UP TO POTTER HEIGHAM PASSING SMALL WATERSIDE CHALETS, SOME WITH EXTREMELY PRETTY FACADES AND GARDENS. IN PARTICULAR LOOK OUT FOR AN UNUSUAL LOOKING COTTAGE ON YOUR LEFT, PURPORTED TO ONCE HAVE BEEN THE TOP OF A HELTER-SKELTER RIDE AT GREAT YARMOUTH!

POTTER HEIGHAM, OF COURSE, IS FAMOUS FOR IT'S BRIDGE (PICTURED ABOVE), "BRIDGE STORES" AND LATHAMS. AT THE BRIDGE YOU MUST WAIT FOR THE PILOT IF YOU WISH TO TRAVEL FURTHER AS THE HEIGHT OF THE BRIDGE IS ONLY 6'9" AT THE CENTRE POINT AT HIGH WATER. ONCE UNDER THE BRIDGE YOU'LL PASS 'HIGH'S MILL' ON YOUR RIGHT. OPPOSITE THIS IS 'CANDLE DYKE' LEADING TO HEIGHAM SOUND AND THEN, VIA A LEFT HAND FORK, HICKLING BROAD. TAKE THE RIGHT FORK FOR 'MEADOW DYKE' WHICH LEADS TO HORSEY MERE.

IF YOU ARE GOING DIRECTLY TO WEST SOMERTON KEEP ON PAST THE TURNING TO CANDLE DYKE AND STAY ON THE MAIN RIVER TO SOMERTON STAITHE.

THURNE

THE LION TEL: (01692) 670796

1/2 MILE FROM THURNE MOUTH - 15 MINUTES
2 MILES TO WOMACK STAITHE - 20 MINUTES

MOORINGS: Approximately 30 side on. There is no charge for mooring on the left hand bank but £3 is requested for those on the right after 4.30 p.m.. The distance to the pub is 100 to 300 yards. Torches may be useful at night.

SUMMER:	11 to 11
WINTER:	5.30 to 11 (All day Saturday)
	Closed Mondays and midday, Jan to March
SUNDAY:	Noon to 11

BEERS: Flowers, Adnams, Wherry, Speckled Hen, Guinness and Guests

LAGERS: Carlsberg, Stella and Fosters.

SPECIALITIES: Chargrilled Steaks. Huge variety of Fish Dishes. Pizzas. Lamb Shank. Bacon and Egg Baguettes. Spicy Bolognese.

SUNDAY LUNCH: Roasts - £6.95.

BAR MEALS: Noon to 2 and 6 to 9

DINING FACILITIES: Seating for 200 inside and out. Times as above. Average cost of three course meal for two with wine: £25.

CARDS: All main cards accepted.

The Lion welcomed new owners in 2005. A purpose built restaurant with smoking and no-smoking areas and function facilities together with a Games Room are now provided.

An old Victorian House with traditional decor and open fires, pool table, amusements and a family room. Soft background music. Dogs are allowed - on leads please. Full facilities for the disabled.

A take away Menu is available and the pub's Gift and Grocery Shop is just across the road. A windmill and a restored windpump stand near the entrance to the dyke leading up to the pub.

POTTER HEIGHAM

THE FALGATE INN   TEL: (01692) 670003

2 MILES FROM WOMACK STAITHE - 20 MINUTES
4 1/2 MILES TO HICKLING AND WEST SOMERTON - 1 HOUR

MOORINGS: Both alongside the bank and in the basin. There is no charge and the distance to the pub is 800 yards. Turn left at the Bridge and go past a small estate. Torches useful at night.

SUMMER:	11 to 3 and 6 to 11
WINTER:	11 to 3 and 6 to 11
SUNDAY:	12 to 3 and 7 to 10.30

BEERS: Tetleys, Greene King IPA, John Smiths, Guinness, Spitfire and Adnams

LAGERS: Stella Artois and Carlsberg

SPECIALITIES: Minted Lamb Chops. Pan Fried Haddock. Spaghetti Bolognese. Steak and Kidney Pie, Curries, Braised Steak. Vegetarian menu. Childrens' Menu.

SUNDAY LUNCH: Roasts - £5.75. Very popular so it may be wise to book ahead

BAR MEALS: Noon to 2 and 6.30 to 9

DINING FACILITIES: Seating for 26. Times as above Average cost of three course meal for two with wine: £35.

CARDS: All main cards accepted. Minimum purchase of £15.

Worth the ten minute walk - so treat yourself! A large old village Inn which was once a Toll House. In the lounge bar the focal point is the fine Tudor fireplace surrounded by horse brasses.

The A La Carte restaurant is intimate and tastefully decorated and it would be a shame to miss out, both on the fabulous food and the Falgate's own excellent wines.

A family room, dartboard and beer garden are provided. Dogs allowed in bar or garden only. En-suite rooms and full English breakfast.

On 27th February 1993 the thatched roof of the pub caught fire and the Falgate only re-opened in November of that year.

WEST SOMERTON

THE LION   TEL: (01493) 393289

4 1/2 MILES FROM POTTER HEIGHAM - 1 HOUR
2 MILES TO HICKLING BROAD AND HORSEY - 30 MINUTES

MOORINGS: There is room for approximately 40 side on along the dyke, bearing right. The distance to the pub is 400 yards going up the hill and around the field. Torches required at night.

SUMMER:	All day from midday.
WINTER:	12 to 3.30 and 6 to 11
SUNDAY:	All day
BEERS:	Greene King IPA, Abbot, Guinness and various Traditional Ales
LAGERS:	Carling Black Label and Guests.
SPECIALITIES:	T-Bone Steaks. Lasagne. King Prawns in Garlic Butter. Mixed Grill. Baguettes.
SUNDAY LUNCH:	Roasts - £5.95. Children also receive jelly or ice-cream and a bottle of 'pop.
BAR MEALS:	11 to 3 and 6 to 9

DINING FACILITIES: Seating for 40. Times as above. Average cost of three course meal for two with wine: £30.

CARDS: All main cards accepted.

A change of ownership in May 2006 meant that we and the new Landlords had a bit of a rush getting up to date before going to print.

Bed and breakfast is now available with three ensuite bedrooms. Call ahead for details.

It is anticipated that a few inner structural changes will take place within the next year or so wthout detracting from The Lion's general charm.

In particular the Lounge Bar will be non-smoking and dogs will only be allowed in the public bar. There will be lunch available on Christmas Day..

HORSEY MERE

THE NELSON HEAD   TEL: (01493) 393378

4 ½ MILES FROM POTTER HEIGHAM - 1 HOUR

MOORINGS: Room for 50 boats anchored side on. There is a small fee and the pub is half a mile from the Staithe.

SUMMER:	All day
WINTER:	All day
SUNDAY:	All day

BEERS:	Greene King, Woodfordes Wherry and Revenge and Speckled Hen.
LAGERS:	Stella Artois and Carling.

SPECIALITIES: Cod, Haddock and Plaice in the Nelsons' Fish Pie. Hot Dogs. Braised Beef. Liver and Bacon. Vegetarian and Childrens' Menus.

SUNDAY LUNCH: Roasts - £7.95 (with *real* Yorkshires!)

BAR MEALS: Noon to 3 and 6 to 9

DINING FACILITIES: Seating for 23. Times as above. Average cost of three course meal for two with wine: £30

CARDS: All main cards accepted.

Tall people duck your heads! The doorway to this old, recently refurbished Freehouse is only 5'.8". Dogs allowed anywhere apart from dining room.

The fireplace in the lounge is large enough to sit in and the bar area has a wealth of brass, copper and ships' memorabilia.

The small, non-smoking, dining room boasts an open fire in Winter and families are welcome. A Marquee bar is available for inclement weather.

Large beer gardens surround the pub which is situated in the centre of a National Trust estate, half a mile from the beach and half a mile from the fully restored Horsey windmill.

HICKLING BROAD

PLEASURE BOAT INN   TEL: (01692) 598211

**4 1/2 MILES FROM POTTER HEIGHAM - 1 HOUR
2 MILES TO WEST SOMERTON OR HORSEY - 30 MINUTES**

MOORINGS: These are plentiful and side on. There is no charge and the pub is 50 to 300 yards away - dependant on where you are moored. £3 overnight if not using the pub.

SUMMER:	All day
WINTER:	All day
SUNDAY:	Noon to 11.30
BEERS:	John Smiths, IPA, Adnams IPA, Courage Dark Mild and Guinness
LAGERS:	Fosters, Carling and 1664
SPECIALITIES:	Beef Madras. Seafood Platter. Pizzas. Mixed Grill. Lasagne. Beef Stroganoff. Spotted Dick.
SUNDAY LUNCH:	Roasts - £4.95
BAR MEALS:	Noon to 3 and 6.30 to 9

DINING FACILITIES: Seating for 50 inside and 70 outside. Noon to 2.30 and 6.30 to 9.30. Typical cost of two course meal for two with wine: £30.

CARDS: Main cards accepted

A change of ownership in 2003. Now a popular family run pub with large and airy rooms and good accesss for the disabled. There is a play area for children and dogs are allowed on leads.

A good A La Carte menu is now available. No-smoking restaurant. Pool Table. Large gardens.

Hickling Broad is the largest lake in Broadlands and was designated as a National Nature Reserve in 1945.

A water trail begins near the pub where it is possible to travel on a replica of a traditional reed-carrying boat known as a "lighter".

THE RIVER WAVENEY - DISTANCES AND TIMINGS

BURGH CASTLE TO GELDESTON

BURGH CASTLE TO ST. OLAVES = 4 1/2 MILES - 30 MINUTES
ST. OLAVES TO NEW CUT = 1/2 MILE - 15 MINUTES
NEW CUT TO SOMERLEYTON = 1 1/2 MILES - 15 MINUTES
SOMERLEYTON TO OULTON BROAD = 5 MILES - 45 MINUTES
OULTON BROAD TO BURGH ST PETER = 3 MILES - 30 MINUTES
BURGH ST PETER TO BECCLES = 6 1/2 MILES - 1 HOUR
BECCLES TO GELDESTON = 2 1/2 MILES - 30 MINUTES

GELDESTON TO BURGH CASTLE

GELDESTON TO BECCLES = 2 1/2 MILES - 30 MINUTES
BECCLES TO BURGH ST PETER = 6 1/2 MILES - 1 HOUR
BURGH ST PETER TO OULTON BROAD = 3 MILES - 30 MINUTES
OULTON BROAD TO SOMERLEYTON = 5 MILES - 45 MINUTES
SOMERLEYTON TO NEW CUT = 1 1/2 MILES - 15 MINUTES
NEW CUT TO ST OLAVES = 1/2 MILE - 15 MINUTES
ST OLAVES TO BURGH CASTLE = 4 1/2 MILES - 30 MINUTES

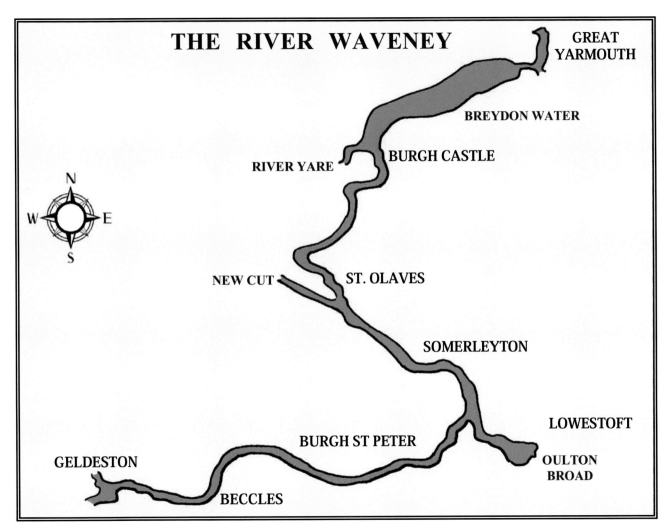

THE RIVER WAVENEY

GREAT YARMOUTH

BREYDON WATER

BURGH CASTLE

RIVER YARE

ST. OLAVES

NEW CUT

SOMERLEYTON

LOWESTOFT

BURGH ST PETER

GELDESTON

BECCLES

OULTON BROAD

N
W E
S

THE RIVER WAVENEY

AT THE BEGINNING OF THIS RIVER LIE THE REMAINS OF BURGH CASTLE. IF YOU WISH TO VISIT FRITTON LAKE COUNTRYWORLD, WHERE THERE IS A CAFE, A NINE HOLE GOLF COURSE, FALCONRY, HORSE AND CART RIDES, FISHING, LAUNCH TRIPS AND HEAVY HORSE STABLES, THE ROAD FROM ST. OLAVES IS BEST.

ALMOST OPPOSITE ST. OLAVES IS THE NEW CUT (BUILT IN 1833), AN ALTERNATIVE ROUTE TO THE RIVER YARE. FURTHER ALONG IS AN IRON SUSPENSION BRIDGE WHICH CONNECTS NORFOLK AND SUFFOLK.

ONCE PAST SOMERLEYTON BEAR LEFT FOR OULTON BROAD. AT LOWESTOFT THERE ARE TOURS TO SEE ROUND THE FISHING TRADE ON TUESDAYS, WEDNESDAYS AND THURSDAYS FROM MID JULY TO MID SEPTEMBER. GOOD BATHING, BINGO, A PAVILION, PARKS, PIERS AND PITCH AND PUTT ARE ALSO WITHIN EASY REACH.

CRUISE ON TO BECCLES (HARBOUR PICTURED ABOVE). BUILT ON SEVERAL LEVELS, BECCLES IS A LOVELY OLD MARKET TOWN WITH A WEALTH OF ANCIENT HOUSES, GOOD SHOPS, SEVERAL PUBS, AND AN OUTSIDE HEATED SWIMMING POOL. THE CHURCH OF ST. MICHAEL, WHERE LORD NELSON'S PARENTS WERE MARRIED IN 1749, CAN BE SEEN AT QUITE A DISTANCE FROM THE RIVER.

BECCLES BRIDGE (HEIGHT AT HIGH WATER - 6'8") SHOULD ONLY BE NAVIGATED AT LOW TIDES. ON THE WAY TO GELDESTON THERE ARE MANY AREAS FOR GOOD FISHING. AT THE TOP OF THE RIVER THE RIGHT FORK LEADS TO GELDESTON VILLAGE.

ST OLAVES

THE BELL INN   TEL: (01493) 488249

4 1/2 MILES FROM BURGH CASTLE - 30 MINUTES
1/2 MILE TO NEW CUT - 10 MINUTES
2 MILES TO SOMERLEYTON – 20 MINUTES

MOORINGS: Room for about 20 boats stern on. There is no charge but watch the current here and keep an eye on the ebb and flow of the river. Distance to pub is 50 to 200 yards.

SUMMER: 11 to midnight (Sunday – Noon to 12)
WINTER: Noon to 3 and 6 to 11 p.m.
SUNDAY: 11 to 10 p.m.

BEERS: Adnams, Broadside and Explorer, Woodfordes Wherry, John Smiths and Guinness.

LAGERS: Fosters and Stella Artois

SPECIALITIES: Beef Chilli. Whole Tail Scampi. Grilled Sausages. Penne Pasta. Liver, Bacon & Sausage Casserole. Childrens' Menu. See www.thebellinn-stolaves.co.uk for all.

SUNDAY LUNCH: £7.75 for 1 course. £10.50 for 2 courses and £13.25 for three. Noon to 8 p.m.

BAR MEALS: Noon to 2.30 and 6.30 to 9

DINING FACILITIES: Seating for 60. 6 to 9 p.m. Average cost of two course meal for two with wine: £30.

CARDS: All main cards accepted.

Under new ownership since June 2005, this is one of Broadlands oldest Inns (circa 1520) with oak beams, genuine brass fittings and copper canopies. Fires are lit whenever "there's a chill in the air". A lovely split-level restaurant overlooks landscaped gardens, a pond, patio and the river beyond. Wines on Tap.

Background and outside music are provided and the service is good. "This Inn welcomes well behaved children and dogs on leads." Special food nights in the winter months.

The remains of 13th Century St. Olaves Priory are situated nearby and Fritton Lake Country World is a mile away from the village.

SOMERLEYTON

THE DUKES HEAD   TEL: (01502) 730281

2 MILES FROM ST OLAVES – 20 MINUTES
5 MILES TO OULTON BROAD STAITHE - 45 MINUTES

MOORINGS: Approximately 30 side on just before Somerleyton Bridge. No charge for the first 24 hours and the distance to the pubs is 200 to 250 yards up the Public Footpath leading from the river. Torches required at night.

SUMMER:	All day
WINTER:	11 to 3.30 and 5.30 to 'closing'.
SUNDAY:	All day

BEERS: Canary, Greene King IPA, Adnams, Orange Wheat, Guinness, Speckled Hen and Guest Beers.

LAGERS: Stella, Fosters, Staropramen, Leffe

SPECIALITIES: Suffolk Sausage and Mash. Lemon Sole. Sea Bass. Roast Chicken. Sirloin. Seafood Omelettes. Raspberry Cheesecake and White Chocolate Sauce . Mmmm.

SUNDAY LUNCH: Roasts: 1 Course - £8.95 – 2, £10.95

BAR MEALS: Noon to 3 and 6.15 to 9.30

DINING FACILITIES: Seating for 30. Times as above. Typical cost of three course meal for two with wine: £45.

CARDS: All cards accepted.

There is a comfortable lounge which boasts a piano. A saloon bar, childrens room and play area are provided plus swings in the large gardens which seat 80 people. Low background music and live music and jazz every few weeks in the Summer months. In the Restaurant weekends are busy so make sure to book ahead for meals

The moorings here have been much improved and there is now a "short cut" through the extensive gardens. Many 'special' events. Dogs welcome.

Wifi *for your Laptop is available here! Plans are in hand for proper disabled facilities. "Wriggle in the Den of Uniquity"!*

OULTON BROAD

THE COMMODORE   TEL: (01502) 565955

**5 MILES FROM SOMERLEYTON - 1 HOUR
3 MILES TO BURGH ST PETER - 30 MINUTES**

MOORINGS: There are 8, side on, at the pub where the charge is £3.50 per night refundable against food purchased inside. Distance to the pub is approximately 200 yards turning left up Commodore Road at the back of the Wherry.

SUMMER:	All day
WINTER:	11 to 3 and 5 to 11
SUNDAY:	Noon to 10.30 in the Summer and Noon to 3 and 5 to 10.30 in the Winter
BEERS:	John Smiths Smooth, Adnams, IPA and Guinness.
LAGERS:	Fosters, Stella and 1664.
SPECIALITIES:	Beef Madras. Cheese and Potato Pie. Mussels. Jacket Potatoes. Vegetarian and Childrens' Menu.
SUNDAY LUNCH:	Roasts - £5.95
BAR MEALS:	Noon to 8.45 p.m.

DINING FACILITIES: Seating for 38 inside with a large dining area outside. Times as above. Average cost of two course meal for two with wine: £17.

CARDS: All major cards except Amex.

Over 100 years old with one large oak beamed bar and small, secluded seating areas. Children are welcome but it is requested that dogs are kept outside. No special facilities for the disabled.

A pub in the true sense of the word. No pool table, no darts and only light background music. With its knot boards and pretty plates the warmth and hospitality are generated by a desire to keep this hostelry as a sociable meeting place for all.

Enjoy unrestricted views over Oulton Broad from the raised balcony dining area and the large tiered gardens reaching down to the patio area at the water's edge. Bar-B-Q's in the summer.

OULTON BROAD

WHERRY HOTEL   TEL: (01502) 516845

5 MILES FROM SOMERLEYTON - 1 HOUR
3 MILES TO BURGH ST PETER – 30 MINUTES

MOORINGS: Numerous stern on. There is a 24 hour mooring charge of £10 for a £5 voucher redeemable on all meals. Distance to the Hotel is 100 to 200 yards.

SUMMER:	11 to 11
WINTER:	11 to 11
SUNDAY:	Noon to 10.30

BEERS: Abbot, Greene King, Guinness and Guest Beers

LAGERS: Carling and Grolsch.

SPECIALITIES: Steak and Kidney. Cajun Chicken. Lasagne. Whole Plaice. Broccoli and Stilton Soup. Childrens' and Vegetarian Menus.

SUNDAY LUNCH: Carvery: £8.50.

BAR MEALS: Noon to 9.30.

DINING FACILITIES: Seating for 120. Noon to 2 and 6 to 9.30. Typical cost of three course meal for two with wine: £35.

CARDS: All main cards accepted.

A large and imposing Hotel with glass and marble decor and a selection of bars, situated on the waterfront. Open plan seating allows for space and comfort. The large glass Conservatory, which overlooks Oulton Broad, is suitable for families.

A pleasant mixture of good service in a sociable and interesting setting. Background music is supplied together with various entertainment during the summer months and there is plenty of seating provided outside. Dogs welcome outside..

Breakfast is available to river travellers Very good facilities for the disabled. Sky TV.

OULTON BROAD

LADY OF THE LAKE

TEL: (01502) 574740

5 MILES FROM SOMERLEYTON - 1 HOUR
3 MILES TO BURGH ST PETER - 30 MINUTES

MOORINGS: Numerous stern on. Distance to the pub is 200 yards across the river bridge by the side of the Wherry. There is a charge of £5.80 stern on and £8.20 side on for 24 hours made by Oulton Broad authority.

SUMMER:	11 to 11 (Weekends open to 2 a.m.)
WINTER:	11 to 11
SUNDAY:	Noon to 10.30

BEERS:	Adnams, IPA, Guinness and John Smiths
LAGERS:	Fosters, Stella and Kronenberg

SPECIALITIES: All day Breakfast. Three Cheese Pasta Bake. Butterfly Chicken. Sirloin and Gammon Steaks. T-Bone Steaks and 'Choice of the Day.'.

SUNDAY LUNCH: £5.95 - Noon to 5 p.m.

BAR MEALS: Noon to 3 and 6 to 9.

DINING FACILITIES: Seating for 60. Times as above. Average cost of three course meal for two with wine: £30.

CARDS: All main cards accepted.

A family pub close to the water with a pleasant patio and gardens. Bar-B-Q's are held during the summer. Special rate meals for senior citizens.

There is one large bar leading into an attractive no-smoking dining area with views over the Broad. Games and a Jukebox are provided and there is a childrens' area. Sorry, no dogs allowed.

Spot the flood level. Ask the landlord what happened in January 1953.

Every Thursday evening, during the Summer, Oulton Broad hosts a power boat race which attracts a large number of visitors.

BURGH ST PETER

THE WAVENEY RIVER CENTRE TEL: (01502) 677599

3 MILES FROM OULTON BROAD - 30 MINUTES
6 ½ MILES TO BECCLES - I HOUR

MOORINGS: Numerous and mostly stern on. There is a charge of £9 for mooring overnight but first 2 hours are free Distance to the Waveney Inn is 50 to 200 yards –

SUMMER:	All day
WINTER:	All day
SUNDAY:	All day

BEERS: Greene King IPA, Ruddles, Abbot and Guest Ales

LAGERS: Carling, Fosters and Stella.

SPECIALITIES: Everything from Filet Steak to Chicken Dishes and Baguettes. Menu changes monthly. Childrens' Menu.

SUNDAY LUNCH: Carvery- £8.95 - Noon to 3

BAR MEALS: 11 to 9.30

DINING FACILITIES: Seating for 90. Times as above. Typical cost of three course meal for two with wine: £35.

CARDS: All main cards accepted

Pleasant service in a quiet and relaxed atmosphere. A general store - renovated in 2005 - and Marina facilities are provided together with an indoor complex featuring a Pool, Sauna, Spa Bath and Gym. Camping facilities, Boat hire and luxury caravan hire are also offered. Live entertainment throughout the summer.

Excellent children's entertainment room. Showers, laundrette boat and cycle hire and fishing. There is a 28 lb Pike which was caught in 1948 on show in the pub.

Good amenities for the disabled. Dogs allowed on leads. Swimming Pool and Laundrette available for a small fee. Showers for £1.

BECCLES

BEAR AND BELLS TEL: (01502) 712291

6 ½ MILES FROM BURGH ST PETER - 1 HOUR
2 1/2 MILES TO GELDESTON - 30 MINUTES

MOORINGS: Plentiful at the main Yacht Basin where the charge is £5.80 stern on and £8.20 side on for 24 hours. A five minute walk, towards the church and into Old Market Square, will take you to the pub.

SUMMER:	11 to 3 and 5.30 to 11
	All day Friday and Saturday
WINTER:	11 to 3 and 5.30 to 11
SUNDAY:	Noon to 3 and 7 to 10.30

BEERS:	Very large range of Adnams and Greene King plus Guest Beers
LAGERS:	Carling Black Label and Stella Artois
SPECIALITIES:	Liver Pate. Pan Fried Salmon. Tiger Prawns. Half a Duck. Sausage Special with Yorkshire Pudding. Childrens' and Vegetarian meals
SUNDAY LUNCH:	Roasts - £6.95 plus Main Menu.
BAR MEALS:	Noon to 2 and 6 to 9

DINING FACILITIES: Seating for 20. Times as above. Typical cost of two course meal for two with wine: £20.

CARDS: All main cards accepted.

One L-shaped bar featuring oak beams, themed World War II pictures and a fascinating collection of jugs and mugs. A 'quiet local pub'.

There is a function room available and the beer gardens are now open since new Landlords took over in 2004 – featuring a lovely Chestnut tree. Non-smoking restaurant. Pub quizzes and folk music nights.

*Interestingly, this Grade II listed building has been **open** as a pub since 1649. In 1815 five horses perished in a disastrous stable fire.*

GELDESTON

THE WHERRY (01508) 518371

2 1/2 MILES FROM BECCLES- 30 MINUTES

MOORINGS: Steer to your right at the fork. Between six and eight side on just before the cut that goes round the old disused railway bridge. There is no charge and the pub is a two minute walk away.

SUMMER: All day
WINTER: Noon to 3 and 7 to 11
SUNDAY: All day

BEERS: Adnams, and Broadside.
LAGERS: Carlsberg and Kronenbourg

SPECIALITIES: Large selection of Fish dishes. Steak and Ale Pie. Gammon. Steaks to order. Childrens' and Vegetarian Menus.

SUNDAY LUNCH: Roasts - £6.95

BAR MEALS: Noon to 2 and 7 to 9

DINING FACILITIES: Seating for 24. Times as above. Typical cost of three course meal with wine: £25.

CARDS: All cards accepted except Amex.

A 16th century building with log fires and a 'real pub' interior with old bench seats and wooden rafters. The lounge has a Swiss Chalet effect.

There is a pretty garden with ample seating, a secluded walled garden and a "secret, non-smoking, restaurant!

Children are welcome as are Dogs - inside and out. There are good facilities for the disabled. "Phat" – a Waveney Valley game is played here – usually on Monday nights.

Fishing is good all round this area, especially for Pike! Canoes for hire just opposite the pub.

GELDESTON

THE LOCKS INN TEL: (01508) 518414

2 1/2 MILES FROM BECCLES - 30 MINUTES

MOORINGS: Fifteen on one side which are free. £2 to £3 per day on the other bank where there is room for twenty five. Distance to the pub is 20 to 50 yards. Torches useful at night.

SUMMER: Noon to closing – every day.
WINTER: Closed Monday and Tuesday. 5 to close Wednesday & Thursday & noon to close Friday, Saturday and Sunday.

BEERS: A great selection of Green Jack Brewery beers such as Grasshopper and Canary. Not to mention "Gone Fishing."
LAGERS: Stella Artois and XXXX.

SPECIALITIES: Friday night is Curry Night. Haddock. Chicken and Leek Pie. Jacket Potatoes. Vegetarian and Childrens' Menu.

SUNDAY LUNCH: Main Menu available.

BAR MEALS: Noon to 2.30 and 6 to 8.30 (Not Sunday evenings)

DINING FACILITIES: Seating for 50. Times as above. Average cost of 2 course meal for 2 with wine. £20

CARDS: Cheques with bankers cards.

One of the oldest pubs in Suffolk, the small tiled and oak beamed bar is still lit by candlelight – any power that is required is supplied by the Inn's own generator.

Extensive renovations have taken place over the past few years and open fires, pub games, folk music nights and a separate childrens room have enhanced this old pub – whilst not detracting from memories of times long past.

Dogs are welcome. Limited facilities for the disabled.

THE RIVERS YARE AND CHET - DISTANCES AND TIMINGS

BERNEY ARMS MILL (BREYDON WATER) TO NORWICH YACHT STATION

BERNEY ARMS MILL TO MOUTH OF NEW CUT = 2 MILES - 20 MINUTES
MOUTH OF NEW CUT TO REEDHAM = 2 1/2 MILES - 25 MINUTES
REEDHAM TO LODDON AND CHEDGRAVE = 5 MILES - 45 MINUTES
REEDHAM TO CANTLEY = 3 MILES - 30 MINUTES
LODDON AND CHEDGRAVE TO CANTLEY = 5 MILES - 45 MINUTES
CANTLEY TO LANGLEY DYKE = 1 MILE - 15 MINUTES
LANGLEY DYKE TO BUCKENHAM = 2 MILES - 30 MINUTES
BUCKENHAM TO ROCKLAND BROAD = 2 MILES - 30 MINUTES
ROCKLAND BROAD TO SURLINGHAM = 3 MILES - 45 MINUTES
SURLINGHAM TO BRAMERTON = 3 MILES - 45 MINUTES
BRAMERTON TO THORPE = 3 MILES - 45 MINUTES
THORPE TO NORWICH YACHT STATION = 2 MILES - 30 MINUTES

NORWICH YACHT STATION TO BERNEY ARMS MILL (BREYDON WATER)

NORWICH YACHT STATION TO THORPE = 2 MILES - 30 MINUTES
THORPE TO BRAMERTON = 3 MILES - 45 MINUTES
BRAMERTON TO SURLINGHAM = 3 MILES - 45 MINUTES
SURLINGHAM TO ROCKLAND BROAD = 3 MILES - 45 MINUTES
ROCKLAND BROAD TO BUCKENHAM = 2 MILES - 30 MINUTES
BUCKENHAM TO LANGLEY DYKE = 2 MILES - 30 MINUTES
LANGLEY DYKE TO CANTLEY = 1 MILE - 15 MINUTES
CANTLEY TO LODDON AND CHEDGRAVE = 5 MILES - 45 MINUTES
CANTLEY TO REEDHAM = 3 MILES - 30 MINUTES
LODDON AND CHEDGRAVE TO REEDHAM = 5 MILES - 45 MINUTES
REEDHAM TO MOUTH OF NEW CUT = 2 1/2 MILES - 25 MINUTES
MOUTH OF NEW CUT TO BERNEY ARMS MILL = 2 MILES - 20 MINUTES

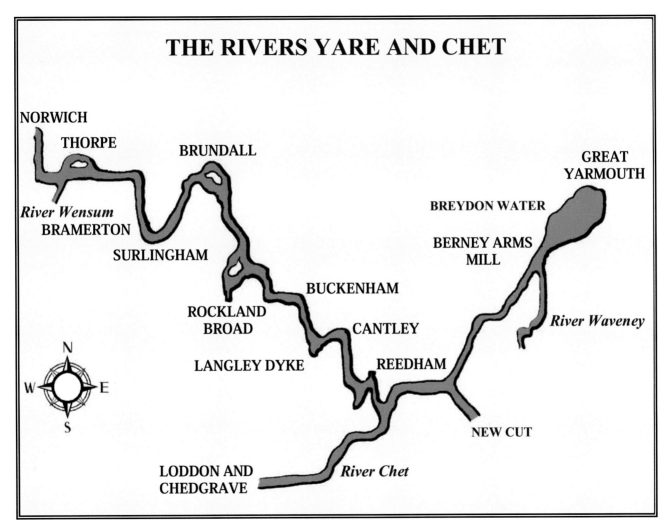

THE RIVERS YARE AND CHET

NORWICH

THORPE

BRUNDALL

GREAT
YARMOUTH

BREYDON WATER

River Wensum
BRAMERTON

BERNEY ARMS
MILL

SURLINGHAM

BUCKENHAM

River Waveney

ROCKLAND
BROAD

CANTLEY

N

LANGLEY DYKE

REEDHAM

W   E

S

NEW CUT

LODDON AND
CHEDGRAVE

River Chet

CROSSING BREYDON WATER AND THE RIVERS YARE AND CHET

CROSSING BREYDON WATER IS NOT AS DAUNTING AS IT LOOKS. ALWAYS CROSS AT LOW TIDES. YOUR ANNUAL TIDE TABLE WILL TELL YOU WHEN THESE ARE. WHEN GOING UNDER BREYDON BRIDGE TAKE CARE TO STEER UNDER THE RED AND WHITE STRIPED TRIANGLES WHICH POINT DOWN TO THE RIVER. IF THREE RED LIGHTS SHOW ON THE BRIDGE KEEP TO THE EXTREME RIGHT HAND CHANNEL. FROM GREAT YARMOUTH TO BERNEY ARMS MILL KEEP BETWEEN THE POSTS AS FOLLOWS:

RED ON YOUR LEFT (PORT) HAND SIDE.
GREEN OR BLACK WITH A WHITE TOP ON YOUR RIGHT (STARBOARD) HAND SIDE.
REVERSE THE ABOVE IF COMING TOWARDS YARMOUTH.

THE CROSSING TAKES APPROXIMATELY 1 HOUR, DEPENDANT ON TIDES. MOORING FEES AT GREAT YARMOUTH, AT THE TIME OF GOING TO PRESS, ARE £11 FOR 24 HOURS.

BERNEY ARMS MILL IS THE TALLEST IN NORFOLK, IS IN FULL WORKING ORDER AND WORTH A VISIT. THE SURROUNDING MARSHES BELONG TO THE R.S.P.B. ONCE PAST THE NEW CUT (A SHORT ROUTE TO THE RIVER WAVENEY) REEDHAM CAN BE SEEN. FURTHER ALONG WATCH OUT FOR REEDHAM CAR FERRY. THIS IS THE LAST WORKING CHAIN FERRY IN EAST ANGLIA.

THE RIVER CHET FLOWS OFF THE YARE AND WILL TAKE YOU TO LODDON AND CHEDGRAVE WHICH ARE ATTRACTIVE MARKET TOWNS.

IF YOU GO PAST THE RIVER CHET, YOU WILL SHORTLY ARRIVE AT CANTLEY WHERE THE FIRST SUGAR BEET FACTORY TO BE BUILT IN THIS COUNTRY IS STILL IN USE. THE RIVER FROM HERE TO THORPE, NEAR NORWICH, IS WIDE AND PLEASANT WITH MANY INTERESTING PUBS ON THE WAY. THORPE BRIDGES ARE 6' AND 6.2" AT HIGH WATER.

REEDHAM

THE SHIP   TEL: (01493) 700287

4 1/2 MILES FROM BERNEY ARMS MILL - 30 MINUTES
5 MILES TO LODDON - 45 MINUTES
3 MILES TO CANTLEY - 30 MINUTES

MOORINGS: Three, side on, by the pub which is very near the railway bridge. There is no charge and the pub is on your 'doorstep', through the pretty gardens. Please keep an eye on the rise and fall of the river if moored overnight.

SUMMER:	11 to 11
WINTER:	11 to 2.30 and 6 to 11 (All day Saturday)
SUNDAY:	All day.

BEERS:	Adnams, Speckled Hen, Broadside, Caffreys and Guinness
LAGERS:	Carling, Grolsch, Stella and Coors.

SPECIALITIES: Pate. Superb Steaks. Different daily specials. Childrens Menu from £2.95. The same Chef for the past 15 years!

SUNDAY LUNCH: Roasts - £6.95.

BAR MEALS: 11 to 2.30 and 6.30 to 9.30

DINING FACILITIES: Seating for 20. Times as above. Average cost of three course meal for two with wine. £28.

CARDS: All main cards accepted.

An interesting collection of miniatures adorn the ceiling of the lounge bar where copper canopied fireplaces and comfortable seating are much in evidence.

The restaurant boasts a very unusual selection of musical instruments and chamber pots!

There is a childrens room with amusements, background music and the occasional jazz group in summer months. Dogs allowed and there is good access for the disabled.

Reedham is an attractive village with numerous cottages, cafes and shops along the water's edge. A well known landmark is the church of St. John the Baptist.

REEDHAM

LORD NELSON

TEL: (01493) 701548

**4 1/2 MILES FROM BERNEY ARMS MILL - 30 MINUTES
5 MILES TO LODDON - 1 HOUR
3 MILES TO CANTLEY - 30 MINUTES**

MOORINGS: Six to eight side on. Double mooring permitted. There is no charge if you are patrons. Distance to the pub is 25 to 50 yards. Please keep an eye on the rise and fall of the river if moored overnight. Torches useful.

SUMMER:	11 a.m. to midnight
WINTER:	Noon to 3 and 6 to 11
SUNDAY:	Noon to 3 and 6 to 11
BEERS:	Greene King IPA, and changing Guest Ales.
LAGERS:	Carling, Stella and "Emma's Lover."!
SPECIALITIES:	Fresh Fish. Steaks. Home-Made Dishes. Chinese Takeaway all year. Afternoon Teas from 3 to 6 p.m.
SUNDAY LUNCH:	Roasts - £6.75 - available noon to 4 p.m.
BAR MEALS:	Noon to 3 and 6 to 9

DINING FACILITIES: Restaurant totally refurbished. Open in the evenings. Typical cost of three course meal for two with wine: £32.

CARDS: All major cards accepted.

Now a Freehouse since a change of ownership in March 2006. There is one large bar with a pleasant dining room which offers lovely views of the river.

Live music is offered 2 to 3 times a week in Summer and once a fortnight in the Winter. Large screen for major sports events. Beer Festival every September.

Children are welcome. Dogs allowed on leads. Limited facilities for the disabled. En-Suite B&B shortly.

Pettits Farm is a ten minute walk from here. Sadly their 'fun bus' does not run anymore.

REEDHAM FERRY

REEDHAM FERRY INN   TEL: (01493) 700429

1 MILE FROM REEDHAM - 20 MINUTES
4 MILES TO LODDON - 45 MINUTES
3 MILES TO CANTLEY – 30 MINUTES

MOORINGS: Plentiful on the pub side of the river. There is no charge and the moorings are exceptionally well kept. Distance to the pub is 100 to 200 yards

SUMMER:	All day (Not Mon. to Wed. see Winter.)
WINTER:	10 to 3 and 5.30 to 11
SUNDAY:	Noon to 10.30.

BEERS: Woodfordes Wherry, Adnams Best, Ferry Special and Broadside. Guinness and various Guest Beers.

LAGERS: Carlsberg, Stella, Carlings and Coors.

SPECIALITIES: Oysters. Lobster. Ferry Fish Stew. Steak and Ale Pie. Suffolk Chicken. Vegetarian and Childrens' Menu.

SUNDAY LUNCH: Roasts: £7.95

BAR MEALS: Noon to 2.30 and 6.30 to 9. Noon to 9 on Sundays.

DINING FACILITIES: Seating for 50. Times as above. Typical cost of three course meal for two with wine: £35.

CARDS: All main cards accepted.

Not included since the 3rd edition and back by popular demand. Two restaurants and a cheerful little split-level bar full of Norfolk memorabilia.

This is a 16th Century Inn with timbered ceilings and large gardens overlooking the river.

There is a large sun room for families with many amusements and the pub is worth a visit for the food alone. Even the bread is from the local bakery.

Good access for the disabled. Dogs allowed. This is where to watch the last working chain ferry in East Anglia.

LODDON

THE SWAN INN   TEL: (01508) 520239

5 MILES FROM REEDHAM - 1 HOUR
5 MILES TO CANTLEY – 1 ½ HOURS

MOORINGS: Plentiful at the Staithe - mostly stern on. There is no charge. Turn left by the Bridge and the Swan is a three minute stroll away, opposite the small Church.

SUMMER:	All day
WINTER:	All day
SUNDAY:	All day

BEERS: Greene King IPA, Woodfordes Wherry, Whitbread Best and Mild, John Smiths and Guinness.
LAGERS: Stella Artois, XXXX, Carlsberg and 1664

SPECIALITIES: Forerib of Pork. Lamb Shanks. Kashmiri. Beef Bourginon. Cumberland Sausages. Roasts every day.

SUNDAY LUNCH: Roasts - £6.25.

BAR MEALS: Noon to 2.30 and 6.30 to 8.30 Tuesday to Sunday inclusive.

DINING FACILITIES: Seating for 20. Times as above. Average cost of three course meal for two with wine: £35.

CARDS: All main cards except Amex

This is a delightful 16th Century Coaching Inn. A non-smoking bar is now provided where you can also dine.

There is a pool table and video machines together with a function room upstairs. Plenty of seating outside for those hot days. Children and dogs are welcome. Good access for the disabled.

Music is supplied by background tapes and a juke box. A market is held every Monday in the pub car park.

The Beer Garden (spoken of in our last edition) is now well and truly open.

LODDON

THE KING'S HEAD   TEL: (01508) 520330

5 MILES FROM REEDHAM- 1 HOUR
5 MILES TO CANTLEY – 1 ½ HOURS

MOORINGS: As before. Turn left and the pub is on your left just before you reach the Swan. Alternatively, from the Staithe go left and through a small wicker gate – follow the path for 200 yards (torches at night) to rear of the pub.

SUMMER:	11 to 11.30
WINTER:	11 to 11.30
SUNDAY:	11 to 11

BEERS: Tetleys, Woodfordes Wherry, Bombardier, IPA, John Smiths and Whitbread Dark Mild
LAGERS: Carlsberg , Carling, Fosters, 1664 and Stella

SPECIALITIES: Mixed Grill. Pork Chops. Rack of Lamb. All Day Breakfast. Tapas. Camembert Fondue. Special Vegetarian food and Childrens' Menu. Everything home cooked.

SUNDAY LUNCH: Roasts - £6.95. 2 courses - £9.95. 3 -£12.

BAR MEALS: 11 to 4 (not Mondays).

DINING FACILITIES: Seating for 40. 6 to 9.30 (not Monday) Average cost of two course meal for two with wine: £26

CARDS: All main cards accepted.

New management from April 2006 in this 400 year old pub where a large open fireplace makes an attractive centrepiece under low timbered ceilings.

The long bar is roomy and comfortable and there are numerous showcases of antiques and memorabilia.

A pool table and Juke Box reside in a separate area where plates and mugs depicting Snooker legends and Jockeys and Horses are on show.

Outside there is a beer garden complete with bird aviary and a play area for children. Dogs welcome.

LODDON

THE ANGEL   TEL: (01508) 520763

5 MILES FROM REEDHAM – 1 HOUR
5 MILES TO CANTLEY – 1 ½ HOURS

MOORINGS: Plentiful at the Staithe - mostly stern on. There is no charge. Turn left by the bridge and the pub is a five minute stroll away - on the left just past the large church.

SUMMER:	11.45 to 3.30 and 6 to 11.30
WINTER:	11.30 to 3.30 and 6 to 11.30
SUNDAY:	Noon to 3 30 and 7 to 10.30
	Closed lunchtime, Monday to Wednesday.

BEERS:	Ansells Bitter, Adnams, IPA, and Tetley.
LAGERS:	Carlsberg and Stella Artois

Please note there is no food available at this pub but it is worth the walk up the hill in order to visit and remember pubs as they used to be.

Run by the same lady for the past six years it feels more like visiting someone's home. We rather liked the difference.

The oldest pub in the village the inside feels more like a private cottage lounge than a pub.

There are three bars with two being on split levels. In the downstairs bar there is an unusual thatched "roof" to the bar area.

During partial renovations over twenty five years ago an ex-landlord requested that his initials be carved for posterity. On looking closely at some of the beams these can still be deciphered.

The original stables and Smoke House can be found at the rear of the pub together with a patio and garden. Dogs are welcome, a pool table is provided and there is a separate family room.

CANTLEY

THE REEDCUTTERS   TEL: (01493) 701099

3 MILES FROM REEDHAM - 30 MINUTES
5 MILES FROM LODDON - 45 MINUTES
5 MILES TO ROCKLAND BROAD - 45 MINUTES

MOORINGS: There are between 20 to 30 side on. There is no charge and the distance to the pub is 50 to 100 yards.

SUMMER:	All day (end May to end September)
WINTER:	11 to 3 and 6 to 11
	11 to 11.30 Friday and Saturday
SUNDAY:	Noon to closing.
BEERS:	Tetleys, Fen Tiger, Guinness and a large selection of changing Real Ales
LAGERS:	Stella Artois and Carling Extra Cold
SPECIALITIES:	All day breakfast. Mixed Grill. Wholetail Scampi. Chilli con Carne. Vegetarian meals. Lite Bites. Childrens' Menu.
SUNDAY LUNCH:	Roasts. £6.95
BAR MEALS:	Noon to 2 and 6 to 9 (extended times during the summer months).

DINING FACILITIES: No-smoking Restaurant seating 28. Noon to 2 and 6 to 9. Average cost of a two course meal for two with wine: £35.

CARDS:	All major cards accepted.

Newly refurbished to a very high standard since the new owners took over in 2004. It is intended that Bed and breakfast will soon be available. Please call ahead.

Open fires and a thatched roof bar. Thursday night is quizz night and the Reedcutter offers various live music on Saturdays.

A beer garden runs alongside the pub and there are seats outside overlooking the river. Children and dogs welcome - "if they don't bite and are on leads."

The Legend reads: "In memory of Mary Flynn who disappeared from this river in 1851." Was she a witch?

ROCKLAND BROAD

THE NEW INN   TEL: (01508) 538403

5 MILES FROM CANTLEY - 45 MINUTES
4 MILES TO SURLINGHAM - 45 MINUTES

MOORINGS: Room for about 15 boats stern on. There is no charge and the pub is 25 to 100 yards away. Torches may be useful at night.

SUMMER:	All day
WINTER:	11 to 3 and 6.30 to 11
SUNDAY:	Noon to 11

BEERS:	Adnams, IPA, John Smith and Guest Ales
LAGERS:	Kronenbourg, Carlsberg and Fosters

SPECIALITIES: Asparagus and Gruyere Flan. Roast Guinea Fowl. Chargrilled Steak Vegetarian food. Mussels.

SUNDAY LUNCH: Roasts - £7.95

BAR MEALS: Noon to 2 and 6 to 8.45 (Not Sunday evening or Mondays)

DINING FACILITIES: Seating for 34. Times as above. Average cost of three course meal for two with wine: £25.

CARDS: All main cards accepted.

An appealing and restful stopover in a quiet and peaceful backwater of the Broads.

An extremely clean interior with historical pictures of the Broads round the walls. Attractive beer gardens and various alterations have greatly enhanced this Inn. There is a no-smoking dining room.

A fine selection of malt and blended whisky is on offer. A family room is provided Dogs welcome, and parties catered for. Ensuite Bed & Breakfast is now available. Please call ahead for details Also it is advisable to call to reserve a table for meals.

BRUNDALL

THE YARE   TEL: (01603) 713786

3 MILES FROM ROCKLAND BROAD – 30 MINUTES
2 MILES TO SURLINGHAM – 15 MINUTES

MOORINGS: Numerous side and stern on and in the boatyards nearby. Distance to the pub is an approximate three minute walk.

SUMMER:	10.30 to 2.30 and 5.30 to 11.30 (Mon-Th.)
	10.30 to midnight (Friday and Saturday)
WINTER:	As above.
SUNDAY:	10.30 to 11-ish.
BEERS:	Abbot, Woodfordes, Bombardier, Courage Mild, Beamish and John Smiths.
LAGERS:	Budweiser and Fosters.
SPECIALITIES:	Trout Almandine. Cod, Plaice and Lemon Sole. Rump and Sirloin Steaks. Liver and Bacon. Hand-made Ice Creams.
SUNDAY LUNCH:	Roasts - £7.95 – 3 courses and coffee. £4.99 - Main Roast only.
BAR MEALS:	Noon to 2 and 6 to 10. Noon to 10 Friday, Saturday and Sunday.

DINING FACILITIES: Seating for 80 anywhere in the pub. Times as above. Average cost of a three course meal for two with wine: £35.

CARDS: All cards accepted.

This large "Broadlands Theme" freehouse is still hosted by Michael Dimarco & Paul Lancaster and has not featured since the second edition.

A family room with amusements, a juke box in the saloon bar and a beer garden outside. A range of souvenirs from Liqueurs and Cigars to Chocolates and T-Shirts are on sale.

In the lounge there is an interesting collection of navigation lights and historical pictures. Log fires in winter. Functions catered for.

The ceiling of the lounge is covered by willow and hazel saplings which are woven into a sheep pen effect known as "waddling."

SURLINGHAM

THE FERRY HOUSE TEL: (01508) 538659

1 MILES FROM SURLINGHAM - 15 MINUTES
2 MILES TO BRAMERTON - 30 MINUTES

MOORINGS: Room for about 20, side and stern on. There is no charge and the distance to the pub is 25 to 100 yards. There may well be a 'ferry boat' from the opposite shore in 2007 run by your hosts.

SUMMER:	All day
WINTER:	Noon to 3 and 6 to 12 – All day Fri & Sat
SUNDAY:	All day

BEERS: Johns Smiths, Adnams, Woolf and constantly changing Local Ales

LAGERS: Fosters and Kronenbourg

SPECIALITIES: Wherryman Bangers. Lamb Chops. Pan Fried chicken. Steak & Ale Pie. Liver and Bacon. Fresh Fish and always fresh Veg.

SUNDAY LUNCH: Main Menu available.

BAR MEALS: Noon to 3. Saturday and Sunday – all day.

DINING FACILITIES: Seating for 30. Times as above. Average cost of three course meal for two with wine. £28.

CARDS: All main cards accepted.

Not featuring in our book for some years this is an 18th century pub which was taken over early in 2006. Look out for great Cappucinos! A walkers paradise all round here and superb for dog lovers.

A pleasant mixture of oak beams, copper, brass, open fireplaces and pictures. A chintzy "country cottage" atmosphere. Live music Friday and Saturday nights in Winter. Reports of ghosts!

The pub has an interesting and chequered history. At one time it was a coal house, then a Court House from which Tithes were paid. It was also an Ice House where ice was sold to fishpackers at Yarmouth and Lowestoft. The chain ferry ceased operation in the late nineteen thirties.

BRAMERTON

THE WOODS END TEL: (01508) 538899

2 MILES FROM SURLINGHAM - 30 MINUTES
4 MILES TO THORPE - 45 MINUTES

MOORINGS: Room for about 20, side on, to your left alongside the pub. There is no charge.

SUMMER: 11 to 11
WINTER: November to February closed lunchtimes except for Weekends. 6.30 to 11 evenings.
SUNDAY: Noon to 10.30 in Summer
Noon to 3 & 7 to 10.30 in Winter

BEERS: Guinness, Boddingtons, Adnams, Woodfordes & Woolf.
LAGERS: Stella Artois and XXXX.

SPECIALITIES: Beef and Guinness. Chilli Bowls. Freshly baked Baguettes. The French/Italian chef has been here for some years now.

SUNDAY LUNCH: Carvery - £6.95

BAR MEALS: Noon to 2 and 7 to 9

DINING FACILITIES: Seating for 40 upstairs and 60 down. Times as above. Average cost of 2 course meal for 2 with wine. £30.

CARDS: All main cards accepted.

A warm welcome at this Freehouse built circa 1885. Pleasant gardens with childrens' play area. No dogs allowed. Live entertainment some weekends. 'Wherryman's Way' Country Walks.

Limited facilities for the disabled. An upstairs 'no-smoking' restaurant is open in the evenings only. A Fish 'n' Chip Shop operates between 4 and 7 on Friday, Saturday and Sunday. Check by telephone first as this may change.

*Ten minutes from Norwich City Centre, bed and breakfast is available at the pub. Indeed, **all** functions are catered for. Call ahead for details. Go to Woods End and "drink the fridge"!*

THORPE

THE RUSHCUTTERS ARMS   TEL: (01603) 435403

4 MILES FROM BRAMERTON - 45 MINUTES
2 MILES TO NORWICH - 30 MINUTES

MOORINGS: Room for about 15 boats moored side on. There is no charge and the pub is 25 to 50 yards away. Navigate carefully under the Bridges and check the tidal ebb and flow if stopping for long.

SUMMER:	11 to 11
WINTER:	11 to 11
SUNDAY:	Noon to 10.30

BEERS: John Smiths Smooth, Guinness, Adnams, Nelsons Revenge and Guest Ales

LAGERS: Fosters, 1664 and Kronenberg

SPECIALITIES: Halibut Supreme. Grilled Lamb Cutlets. Sausage and Mash. Lemon Sole. Mixed Grill. Mussels. Childrens' Menu.

SUNDAY LUNCH: Roasts (until they run out) - £7.95 plus Main Menu

BAR MEALS: 11 to 10. Noon to 9.30 Sunday

DINING FACILITIES: Seating anywhere in pub. Times as above Typical cost of two course meal for two with wine: £32.

CARDS: All main cards and ATM machine.

Thorpe St. Andrew is known as the Richmond of Norfolk and, here, in this spacious hostelry everything is provided for the family.   Good facilities for those with mobility problems.

The bars and parts of the dining areas, with their oak beams and open fires in winter, overlook the river and there is a vast Patio area outside, from where you can watch the world go by.

In the 18th Century a rail crash resulted in the place being used as a temporary morgue. Before the Rushcutters was a public house it was a Coaching Inn and before that a Monastery. The ghost of a monk is still frequently seen!

THORPE ST ANDREW

THE BUCK INN   TEL: (01603) 434682

4 MILES FROM BRAMERTON – 45 MINUTES
2 MILES TO NORWICH – 30 MINUTES

MOORINGS: Room for about 15 boats side on. There is no charge and the pub is 25 to 50 yards away across the green. Carefully under the Bridge and watch the tides.

SUMMER: 11 to midnight.
WINTER: 11 to midnight.
SUNDAY: Noon to midnight.

BEERS: Adnams, Wherry IPA, Spitfire, Guinness, John Smiths and Guest Ales.
LAGERS: Carlsberg, Stella Artois and 1664.

SPECIALITIES: Whitebait. Steak and Kidney. Chilli. Chargrilled Chicken. Gammon. Lamb Shank. Specials Board. Vegetarian and Childrens' Menu.

SUNDAY LUNCH: Roasts - £5.95 plus Main Menu.

BAR MEALS: Noon to 2.30 and 6 to 9 (Mon. to Thurs.) Noon to 2.30 and 6 to 9.30 Fri. and Sat.) Noon to 9 on Sundays.

DINING FACILITIES: Seating available anywhere in pub. Times as above. Average cost of two course meal for two with wine: £28.

CARDS: All main cards accepted.

Built in 1583, comfort and relaxation are the watchwords here. Install yourself in one of the three split-level rooms which are all served by the same long bar..

The service is cordial and animated and the background music is not too intrusive – although there is a working Grammaphone!

Copper kettles, pewter tankards, Batey Jars and old beer bottles sit snugly on the beamed rails. Children welcome. Access for the disabled. Dogs allowed outside in the pretty courtyard.

THORPE

THE RIVER GARDEN TEL: (01603) 703900

4 MILES FROM BRAMERTON - 45 MINUTES
2 MILES TO NORWICH - 30 MINUTES

MOORINGS: Room for three side on outside the pub (free if dining) and plenty a little further down along the river bank. Carefully under either Bridge and watch the tides. This pub is totally non-smoking since May 2006!

SUMMER:	All day
	Monday to Wednesday 11 a.m. to late.
	Thursday to Saturday 11 a.m. to 1 a.m.
WINTER:	As above.
SUNDAY:	Noon to 11
BEERS:	Boddingtons and Woodforde plus Guinness and Guest Ales.
LAGERS:	Fosters and Stella Artois
SPECIALITIES:	Thai style Chicken. Lamb Shank. Norfolk Sausages. Baked Salmon. Pasta. Noodles. Salads.
SUNDAY LUNCH:	Roasts - £8.95
BAR MEALS:	Noon to 10.

DINING FACILITIES: Seating anywhere in pub or no-smoking restaurant. Times as above. Typical cost of two course meal for two with wine: £35.

CARDS: All main cards accepted.

THORPE

THE TOWN HOUSE TEL: (01603) 700600

4 MILES FROM BRAMERTON - 45 MINUTES
2 MILES TO NORWICH - 30 MINUTES

MOORINGS: Room for four to five boats side on outside the hotel. There is no charge and entrance is via the gardens. Carefully under the Bridge and watch the tides.

SUMMER:	All day
WINTER:	All day
SUNDAY:	Noon to 10.30
BEERS:	Green King IPA, Marstons Pedigree, Tetleys and Guinness.
LAGERS:	Heineken, Stella, Carlsberg and Carling.
SPECIALITIES:	Pork Belly. Mixed Grill. Sea Bass. Seasonal Selections as befits Beefeater
SUNDAY LUNCH:	Roasts - £6.95
BAR MEALS:	Noon to 9 (Sunday to Friday) Noon to 10 p.m. Saturday.

DINING FACILITIES: Restaurant seating for 120. 12 to 2 and 5.30 to 10. Saturday – Noon to 10.30. Sunday - Noon to 9. Typical cost of three course meal for two with wine: £30.

CARDS: All main cards accepted.